BUDGET JUSTIFICATIONS

The United States
Department of the Interior

JUSTIFICATIONS

and Performance Information
Fiscal Year 2015

OFFICE OF
THE SOLICITOR

TABLE OF CONTENTS

OFFICE OF THE SOLICITOR
ORGANIZATIONAL CHART

SOLICITOR

PRINCIPAL DEPUTY SOLICITOR

- Administration Director

DEPUTY SOLICITOR ENERGY & MINERAL RESOURCES
- Mineral Resources Associate Solicitor

DEPUTY SOLICITOR PARKS & WILDLIFE
- Parks & Wildlife Associate Solicitor

DEPUTY SOLICITOR INDIAN AFFAIRS
- Indian Affairs Associate Solicitor
- Indian Trust Litigation Office Director

DEPUTY SOLICITOR WATER RESOURCES
- Land & Water Resources Associate Solicitor

DEPUTY SOLICITOR PUBLIC LANDS
- Ethics Office Director

DEPUTY SOLICITOR GENERAL LAW
- General Law Associate Solicitor
- Collaborative Action & Dispute Resolution Senior Counsel
- Front Office support staff

Regional and Field Solicitors:

- Alaska Region Anchorage, AK Regional Solicitor
- Pacific NW Region Portland, OR Regional Solicitor
  - Boise, ID Field Solicitor
- Pacific SW Region Sacramento, CA Regional Solicitor
  - San Francisco, CA Field Solicitor
- Intermountain Region Salt Lake, UT Regional Solicitor
  - Phoenix, AZ Field Solicitor
- Rocky Mt. Region Denver, CO Regional Solicitor
  - Billings, MT Field Solicitor
- Southwest Region Albuquerque, NM Regional Solicitor
  - Tulsa, OK Field Solicitor
- Northeast Region Boston, MA Regional Solicitor
  - Twin Cities, MN Field Solicitor
  - Pittsburgh, PA Field Solicitor
- Southeast Region Atlanta, GA Regional Solicitor
  - Knoxville, TN Field Solicitor

GENERAL STATEMENT

The Office of the Solicitor (SOL, Office) maintains the focal mission of inspiring high ethical standards and providing quality legal counsel and advice to the Department and its Bureaus and Offices. The Office supports the Department of the Interior's broad mission by performing the legal work of the Department, managing Interior's Ethics Office and resolving Freedom of Information Act (FOIA) Appeals. The Office is the premier environmental and natural resources legal organization, and through its efforts the Department leads the country in conservation and management of our public natural and cultural resources.

The Office provides advice, counsel, and legal representation to the Immediate Office of the Secretary, the Assistant Secretaries, and all other bureaus and offices overseen by the Secretary. The advice provided by the Office impacts nearly every program within the Secretary's jurisdiction. The Office coordinates with the Department of Justice to address issues before Federal courts.

The Office is organized into the Immediate Office of the Solicitor, the Ethics Office, five legal divisions, an administrative division, and sixteen regional and field offices located throughout the United States.

The Solicitor is the chief attorney for Interior. The Solicitor is assisted by a Principal Deputy, six Deputy Solicitors, Senior Counselors, an Ethics Director, six Associate Solicitors, eight Regional Solicitors, and a staff of more than three hundred attorneys and four hundred total employees.

More than half of the attorneys are assigned to regional and field offices located as far west as Anchorage, Alaska and as far east as Boston, Massachusetts. The other attorneys are assigned to divisions located at headquarters in Washington, D.C.

The Office of the Solicitor's FY 2015 budget focuses on supporting the Department of the Interior's efforts to improve efficiency and effectiveness in its conservation and land management missions, as well as its commitments to American Indians, Alaska Natives and affiliated insular communities. The FY 2015 budget allows the Office to continue to improve management practices and manage the Ethics Office for maximum effectiveness.

THE PRESIDENT'S MANAGEMENT AGENDA:

The Department of the Interior supports the President's Management Agenda to cut waste and implement a government that is more responsive and open. The Office of the Solicitor budget supports the Department's plan to build upon the Accountable Government Initiative through a set of integrated enterprise reforms designed to support collaborative, evidence-based resource management decisions; efficient Information Technology (IT) Transformation; optimized programs, business processes, and facilities; and a network of innovative cost controlling measures that leverage strategic workforce alignment to realize an effective 21st Century Interior organization.

The FY 2015 President's Budget Request includes $28,000 for the Office of the Solicitor participation in the Department's IT Transformation efforts through the Department's Working Capital Fund. These funds will support IT Transformation project-level planning and coordination, which is the first of several phases necessary for the implementation of enterprise IT services across the Department.

MANAGEMENT'S CHALLENGES:

The Office of the Solicitor's FY 2015 budget request was formulated with full consideration of the tight limits on discretionary spending. The request anticipates the continuation of a reduced workforce for the Office that still enables the Office to continue to promote an ethical culture throughout the Department and to maintain much of the established level of legal services to the Department. The Office must continually examine and prioritize meeting the needs of an ever increasing workload.

The Office has undergone continual and significant management reform over the past several years. Management reforms have been primarily driven by: (1) the need to provide early and continuous legal counsel on the development of new programs in priority areas such as renewable energy, restoration of tribal homelands, and youth engagement in the stewardship of natural and cultural resources, while maintaining the Office's established level of service to the existing programs in the rest of the Department; (2) the ability to be nimble in meeting urgent and emergent needs for legal counsel in addressing DOI's responses to severe or emergency resource management challenges; (3) the need to provide ongoing expert legal services in defending the Department in Federal court and administrative litigation; (4) the need to provide timely and comprehensive advice and counsel on the development of new legislation and ensuring that the Department's testimony and views on legislation are legally sound; (5) the need to provide thorough planning and substantive support in rulemaking activities throughout the Department; and (6) the need to provide legal services to support and advance open Government initiatives.

The Office must provide early and continuous guidance in new priority areas to ensure that developing programs are grounded in established legal principles and precedents. The Office must be able to focus on priority areas such as conventional and renewable energy development, including improved management of Federal oil and gas resources; Information Technology Transformation; civil enforcement of pollution-control laws; climate change adaptation; refocused implementation of the Endangered

Species Act; Strengthening Tribal Nations; Engaging the Next Generation; Ensuring Healthy Watersheds and Sustainable, Secure Water Supplies; Building Landscape-Level Understanding of Our Resources; and executing the Open Government Directive, all without diminishing the level of service provided to existing and established Departmental programs.

The Office must remain ready when called upon to assist the Secretary to meet challenges presented by unusual circumstances, such as severe drought conditions in California and their impact on DOI program management. The Office is cognizant of the need to balance urgent and emergent needs with routine or regular delivery of services.

MANAGEMENT'S STRATEGIES:

In planning for FY 2014 and 2015, the Office's management team led a series of internal dialogues and management assessments, including: (1) committing to and working with the bureaus to identify and plan for prioritizing legal work to support program priorities; (2) assessing the level of legal services we provide and determining how to deliver them more efficiently; (3) assessing how we might reorganize ourselves around specific substantive areas of work to realize efficiencies; (4) looking at staffing models to identify hiring priority improvements; and (5) offering VERA opportunities to employees to assist us in reshaping our workforce to improve its sustainability. By engaging in these efforts, the Office has made significant strides in addressing our challenges and the FY 2015 budget will ensure the Office can continue to make progress in these areas.

Addressing Emerging Priorities

The Office of the Solicitor will continue to have wide-ranging demands for legal services in FY 2015 in established practice areas, such as the development of the offshore oil and gas five-year plan, continued permitting of conventional and renewable energy projects, administration of tribal and individual Indian resources, statutorily required decision-making under the Endangered Species Act, and a host of other land management and scientific programs. In addition, the Office will face many new and complex demands for legal services as the Department ramps up efforts in programs such as the promotion of tribal self-governance and trust land acquisitions; the Cobell land buy-back program; the transformation of the Department's information technology, including the continued development of new tools to provide landscape level understanding of our natural and cultural resources; the enhanced engagement of youth in natural and cultural resource programs; the development of more efficient permitting systems for natural resource extraction and renewable energy production; and the development of more effective land and water management strategies to adapt to climate change and other stresses on federally administered lands and projects.

While maintaining excellence in the delivery of established legal services, the Office is also facing urgent needs to support DOI programs affected by severe drought conditions this year. For example, the Office must be prepared to deliver up-to-the-minute advice on bureaus' programmatic needs, such as: water delivery contract interpretation, operational changes affecting the status of biological opinions, river restoration program needs, and drought-related legislation. These are but a few of the time-sensitive matters where the Office may be called upon to render immediate advice. In any given year, the Office may face more than one significant and far-reaching emergency situation altering the course of planned resource management, necessitating that the Office be able to step in and assist the bureaus to ensure sound programmatic decisions are made.

In addition to the expected growing workload in a wide variety of natural and cultural resource areas, the Office expects a growing workload in contracting and personnel administration as the Department's various Bureaus undertake efforts to streamline their operations. The Office also expects more legal service demands from the Department in FY 2015 related to statutorily required agency processes and decisions under the Outer Continental Shelf Lands Act, the Endangered Species Act, and the National Environmental Policy Act.

Making Ethics a Priority

In Fiscal Year 2013, the Department of the Interior's Ethics Office provided ethics training to thousands of Departmental employees via a video broadcast discussing the history of the ethics laws to which Federal employees must adhere. The video, introduced by Secretary of the Interior Sally Jewell, gave context to employees regarding the complex ethics laws, allowing them to better understand the importance of upholding high ethical standards in carrying out the Department's mission. The video was widely received as the most effective ethics training employees had ever received. In addition, the Ethics Office held an Ethics Summit in which all headquarters staff and eleven bureau deputy ethics counselors participated. The Summit included an executive leadership roundtable on how to communicate ethics issues to senior leaders. In addition, the Summit provided training for ethics staff on how to deliver more thorough ethics advice and counsel to the Department's employees. While the Ethics Office is in part a compliance office, it is not an enforcement or investigatory office. In addition to compliance and program management, its mission is prospective: helping employees think through potential ethics issues, including conflicts of interest, before taking action. The 2013 training and the Ethics Summit are examples of the Office's commitment to cultivating an ethical culture at the Department of the Interior.

FISCAL YEAR 2015 BUDGET REQUEST OVERVIEW

The FY 2015 President's Budget request for the Office of the Solicitor is $65,800,000, level with the Office's FY 2014 Enacted budget. The request includes a reduction of $717,000 in legal services for workforce planning to fund $717,000 for fixed costs.

The Office developed a 2015 budget that focuses on supporting the Department of the Interior's efforts to improve the efficiency and effectiveness of Department-wide programs by delivering the highest quality legal services to Interior.

The following table illustrates the 2013 Actual, the 2014 Enacted, and the 2015 Budget Request.

TOTAL 2015 BUDGET REQUEST
(Dollars in Thousands)

Budget Authority	2013 Actual	2014 Enacted	2015 President's Budget
Appropriation Total	62,728	65,800	65,800
FTE Direct	327	333	328
FTE Reimbursable	71	69	69
FTE Allocation	20	20	20
FTE Total	418	422	417

Budget at a Glance
(Dollars in Thousands)

Appropriation: Salaries & Expenses	2013 Actual	2014 Enacted	Fixed Costs	Program Changes	2015 President's Budget
Legal Services	45,974	59,658	150	-717	59,091
Workforce Planning				[-717]	
General Administration	15,259	4,647	324	0	4,971
Ethics Office	1,495	1,495	243	0	1,738
TOTAL, SOL	**62,728**	**65,800**	**717**	**-717**	**65,800**

Summary of Requirements
(Dollars in Thousands)

Salaries & Expenses	2013 Actual	2014 Enacted			Program Changes (+/-)		2015 President's Budget		Change from PY	
	Amount	Total FTE	Amount	Fixed Costs & Related	FTE	Amount	FTE	Amount	FTE	Amount
Legal Services	45,974	301	59,658	+150	-5	-717	296	59,091	-5	-567
General Administration	15,259	24	4,647	+324	+0	+0	24	4,971	+0	324
Ethics	1,495	8	1,495	+243	+0	+0	8	1,738	+0	243
TOTAL, SOL	**62,728**	**333**	**65,800**	**+717**	**-5**	**-717**	**328**	**65,800**	**-5**	**0**

Summary of Changes
(Dollars in Thousands)

Appropriation: Salaries and Expenses	FTE	Amount	FTE	Amount
FY 2014 Enacted			333	65,800
Fixed Costs and related changes:				
Calendar Year 2014 & 2015 Pay Raise	0	+488		
Employer Share of Federal Health Benefit Plans	0	+25		
Departmental Working Capital Fund	0	-389		
Worker's Compensation Payments	0	+556		
GSA Rental Payments	0	+37		
Program changes:				
Workforce Planning	-5	-717		
Total program changes			-5	0
FY 2015 President's Budget Request			328	65,800

Office of the Solicitor
Justification of Fixed Costs
(Dollars In Thousands)

Fixed Cost Changes and Projections	2014 Total	2014 to 2015 Change
Pay Raise		+488
The change reflects the salary impact of a programmed one percent pay raise increases as proposed in the Circular A-11.		
Employer Share of Federal Health Benefit Plans		+25
The change reflects expected increases in employer's share of Federal Health Benefit Plans.		
Departmental Working Capital Fund	3,891	-389
The change reflects expected changes in the charges for centrally billed Department services and other services through the Working Capital Fund. These charges are displayed in the Budget Justification for Department Management.		
Worker's Compensation Payments	240	+556
The adjustment is for changes in the costs of compensating injured employees and dependents of employees who suffer accidental deaths while on duty. Costs for the BY will reimburse the Department of Labor, Federal Employees Compensation Fund, pursuant to 5 U.S.C. 8147(b) as amended by Public Law 94-273.		
Unemployment Compensation Payments	8	+0
The adjustment is for projected changes in the costs of unemployment compensation claims to be paid to the Department of Labor, Federal Employees Compensation Account, in the Unemployment Trust Fund, pursuant to Public Law 96-499.		
Rental Payments	8,143	+37
The adjustment is for changes in the costs payable to General Services Administration (GSA) and others resulting from changes in rates for office and non-office space as estimated by GSA, as well as the rental costs of other currently occupied space. These costs include building security; in the case of GSA space, these are paid to Department of Homeland Security (DHS). Costs of mandatory office relocations, i.e. relocations in cases where due to external events there is no alternative but to vacate the currently occupied space, are also included.		
Total Fixed Costs Changes		+717

APPROPRIATION LANGUAGE

SALARIES AND EXPENSES

For necessary expenses of the Office of the Solicitor, $65,800,000.
(Department of the Interior, Environment, and Related Agencies Appropriations Act, 2014.)

APPROPRIATION LANGUAGE CITATION

Appropriation: **Salaries and Expenses**

For necessary expenses of the Office of the Solicitor.

43 U.S.C. § 1455

43 U.S.C. § 1455 provides that, on and after June 26, 1946, the legal work of the Department of the Interior shall be performed under the supervision and direction of the Solicitor of the Department of the Interior, who shall be appointed by the President with the advice and consent of the Senate.

GENERAL ADMINISTRATION ACTIVITY

Activity: General Administration

(Dollars in Thousands)

	2013 Actual	2014 Enacted	2015			Change from 2014 (+/-)
			Fixed Costs & Related Changes (+/-)	Program Changes (+/-)	Budget Request	
General Administration	15,259	4,647	+ 324	0	4,971	+ 324
FTE	*59*	*24*	*0*	*0*	*24*	*0*

The 2015 budget request for General Administration is $4,971,000 and 24 FTE.

<u>GENERAL ADMINISTRATION PROGRAM OVERVIEW</u>:

Division of Administration: Under the direction of an Associate Solicitor, the Division of Administration is responsible for providing and coordinating all management and administrative services needed by the Office. Responsibilities in the Division of Administration include: organizational, strategic, and performance planning; program evaluation; budget and accounting; human resources management; employee development and training; space and property management; procurement services; IT planning and services; and records management.

LEGAL SERVICES ACTIVITY

Activity: Legal Services

(Dollars in Thousands)

	2013 Actual	2014 Enacted	2015			Change from 2014 (+/-)
			Fixed Costs & Related Changes (+/-)	Program Changes (+/-)	Budget Request	
Legal Services	45,974	59,658	+ 150	- 717	59,091	- 567
FTE	260	*301*	*0*	*- 5*	*296*	*- 5*

Summary of 2015 Program Changes for Legal Services

Request Component	($000)	FTE
Program Changes:		
• Workforce Planning	-717	-5
TOTAL Program Changes	**-717**	**-5**

The 2015 budget request for Legal Services is $59,091,000 and 296 FTE, a program decrease of -$717,000 and -5 FTEs from the 2014 Enacted level.

Workforce Planning (-$717,000/ -5 FTEs) – The Office of the Solicitor requests a reduction of $717,000 for FTEs. The Office will realize a 5 FTE reduction in FY 2015 through workforce planning and position management. While the legal work for the Department is increasing, the Office recognizes the need for tighter limits on discretionary spending. The Office will coordinate with client-bureaus and offices to balance legal work demands and prioritize their requests for attorney involvement.

LEGAL SERVICES PROGRAM OVERVIEW

The responsibility of the Legal Services program is to effectively manage the legal work to support the top priorities of the Secretary and the bureaus. Among these legal services are representation in litigation, both administrative and judicial; preparation of legal opinions; legal review of legislation, regulations, contracts, and other documents; and informal legal counsel to clients on a continual basis in a wide variety of circumstances.

The Office of the Solicitor consists of a headquarters organization in Washington, D.C., and regional and field offices in 16 locations throughout the United States. The Solicitor is the chief attorney for Interior and the principal legal adviser to the Secretary. The Solicitor directs the Office's professional staff and is responsible for the legal work provided to Interior.

The Washington, D.C. office is organized into the Immediate Office of the Solicitor, which includes six Deputy Solicitors with subject matter oversight, the Ethics Office, five major legal divisions, and an administrative division as detailed below. Each legal division is headed by an Associate Solicitor who is directly responsible to the Solicitor and Deputy Solicitor. Attorneys under the supervision of Associate Solicitors render legal services for Interior's programs. The field organization of the Solicitor's Office is divided into eight regions, as detailed below. Each region is headed by a Regional Solicitor who is directly responsible to the Solicitor and Principal Deputy Solicitor.

HEADQUARTERS

Immediate Office of the Solicitor

Ethics Office

Division of Parks and Wildlife

Division of General Law

Division of Indian Affairs

Division of Land and Water Resources

Division of Mineral Resources

Division of Administration

REGION	REGIONAL OFFICES	FIELD OFFICES
Alaska	Anchorage, Alaska	----
Southeast	Atlanta, Georgia	Knoxville, Tennessee
Northeast	Boston, Massachusetts	Pittsburgh, Pennsylvania Twin Cities, Minnesota
Intermountain	Salt Lake City, Utah	Phoenix, Arizona
Rocky Mountain	Denver, Colorado	Billings, Montana
Pacific Northwest	Portland, Oregon	Boise, Idaho
Pacific Southwest	Sacramento, California	San Francisco, California
Southwest	Albuquerque, New Mexico	Tulsa, Oklahoma

PROGRAM AND ORGANIZATION DESCRIPTIONS

The majority of the Office's resources are devoted to the defense of a wide range of litigation against the United States, both administrative and judicial, and to other "nuts-and-bolts" legal services, ensuring that Interior's agencies carry out their responsibilities in accordance with the law. In most judicial litigation, SOL attorneys actively assist or are co-counsel with attorneys from DOJ. In some judicial litigation and all administrative litigation, Office attorneys represent Interior without assistance from DOJ.

The Office also provides everyday legal service assistance in drafting and reviewing legislation, proposed and final regulations, contracts, memoranda of agreement, decisions, agreements, leases, rights-of-way, title documents, and other legal instruments, as well as providing both written and oral legal advice on a constant flow of legal questions. Some of these questions arise from such generic statutes as the Administrative Procedure Act, Freedom of Information Act, Privacy Act, Federal Advisory Committee Act (FACA), Federal Tort Claims Act, Civil Service Reform Act, the Civil Rights Acts, and the Rehabilitation Act, while other questions arise from the many specific statutes applicable to Interior's program areas in which the Office's attorneys and paralegals have developed significant expertise.

In addition to this essential baseline of legal work, the Office engages in a significant number of special legal projects, providing critical legal support for Interior's key initiatives. The legal staff assists the bureaus in responding to congressional direction in appropriations and substantive legislation. The Office advises the bureaus on legal options for streamlining processes and improving program management and implementing plans to carry out departmental goals. Finally, the Office assists the bureaus in responding to Inspector General, congressional, judicial, and public FOIA requests, as well as subpoenas for documents.

In addition to the Immediate Office of the Secretary and the offices of the Assistant Secretaries, client-representatives include the following bureaus and offices within Interior:

Bureau of Indian Affairs (BIA)
Bureau of Indian Education (BIE)
Bureau of Land Management (BLM)
Bureau of Reclamation (BOR)
Fish and Wildlife Service (FWS)
Bureau of Ocean Energy Management (BOEM)
Bureau of Safety and Environmental Enforcement (BSEE)
National Park Service (NPS)
National Resource Damage Assessment and Restoration Program (NRDAR)
Office of Surface Mining Reclamation and Enforcement (OSM)
United States Geological Survey (USGS)
Policy, Management and Budget (PMB)
Office of Aviation Services (OAS)
Office of Chief Information Officer (OCIO)
Office of Civil Rights (OCR)
Office of Environmental Policy and Compliance (OEPC)
Office of Historical Trust Accounting (OHTA)
Office of Indian Trust Transition (OITT)
Office of Insular Affairs (OIA)
Office of the Special Trustee (OST)
Indian Arts and Crafts Board (IACB)
Federal Subsistence Board (FSB)
Exxon Valdez Trustee Council

Client-representative specific narratives are omitted for those bureaus and offices where the legal services provided are predominantly generic, that is, relating to personnel, procurement, FOIA, and other statutes of general applicability to all bureaus and offices.

ORGANIZATIONAL DESCRIPTIONS

The **Immediate Office of the Solicitor** includes the Solicitor, Principal Deputy Solicitor, six Deputy Solicitors, Special Assistants, Senior Counselors, and supporting secretarial staff. The Immediate Office is responsible for managing and directing all the legal work in the Office.

The **Division of General Law** is responsible for legal matters related to procurement, patents, and tort claims; insular areas; equal employment opportunity, labor law, and other personnel matters; and administrative and other general legal issues, including legislative and appropriations issues not assigned to another division. In addition, the Division provides legal assistance and counsel to the Assistant Secretary - Policy, Management and Budget and to the Endangered Species Committee. The Division also manages the Department's FOIA and Privacy Act (PA) appeals program. The Division has an Associate Solicitor, three branches, each headed by an Assistant Solicitor, and one office headed by a branch chief.

(1) The Branch of Personnel Litigation and Civil Rights has responsibility for defensive employment litigation before the Merit Systems Protection Board, Equal Employment Oppurtunity Commission, Federal Labor Relations Authority, and in assisting the Department of Justice in employment cases in Federal court. The litigation practice involves, among other things, Chapters 43 and 75 of Title 5 of the U.S. Code, Title VII of the Equal Employment Opportunity Act, Rehabilitation Act, Age Discrimination in Employment Act, Veteran's Employment Opportunity Act, Uniformed Services Employment and Reemployment Rights Act, Veterans Employment Oppurtunities Act, Whistleblower Protection Act, the Family Medical Leave Act, and the Fair Labor Standards Act. A substantial portion of the practice of the Branch is devoted to providing counseling and review on employment matters to the Office of the Secretary and the Bureau Offices located in Washington, D.C., providing legal engagement in personnel policy and Title VI policy matters, and ensuring consistency in legal services throughout the Office of the Solicitor.

(2) The Branch of Acquisitions and Intellectual Property has responsibility for: legal matters related to Interior acquisition and procurement functions including all related litigation; use of revolving and franchise funds; interagency agreements, grants and cooperative agreements; claims based on the Federal Tort Claims Act, the Military Personnel and Civilian Employees Claims Act; patents, copyrights, trademarks, rights in data, and other forms of intellectual property; legal support of fast-track contracting and assistance under the American Recovery and Reinvestment Act; claims relating to agreements; and contracts under the Indian Self Governance and Self Determination Acts. A portion of the practice of the Branch is devoted to providing early legal engagement, counseling and review for diverse clients; while ensuring consistency in general legal services throughout the Office of the Solicitor.

(3) The Branch of General Legal Services has responsibility for legal matters and litigation related to budget, financial management, legal ethics, FOIA, records management, electronic data management, partnerships, the FACA, the PA, rulemaking, and other administrative law matters, internal delegations of authority, departmental law enforcement policies, insular areas, and all other related and general matters not specifically the responsibility of any other branch or division. A portion of the practice of the Branch is devoted to providing early legal engagement, counseling and review for diverse clients; while ensuring consistency in general legal services throughout the Office of the Solicitor.

(4)   The Freedom of Information Act and Privacy Act Appeals Office has responsibility for FOIA and PA appeals and coordinates and manages the Department's FOIA and PA appeals program. The Office is headed by the Departmental FOIA/PA Appeals Officer who has authority to directly issue appeal decisions for matters involving procedural issues not requiring legal review. An example of the type of such an appeal would be one alleging that a bureau did not conduct an adequate search of its files.

The **Division of Indian Affairs** is responsible for legal matters related to the programs and activities of the Bureau of Indian Affairs and the Bureau of Indian Education. In addition, the Division provides legal assistance and counsel to the Assistant Secretary - Indian Affairs. The Division has an Associate Solicitor and four branches, each headed by an Assistant Solicitor.

(1)   The Branch of Water and Power has responsibility for legal matters related to BIA programs and activities with respect to water rights held in trust by the United States for Indian Tribes and allottees, including adjudications and Congressional settlements of Indian water rights; license applications before the Federal Energy Regulatory Commission and hydroelectric power projects that affect Indian reservations and resources; and the operation and maintenance of BIA irrigation projects.

(2)   The Branch of Trust Responsibility has responsibility for advising the Secretary in the Secretary's capacity as trustee over lands and minerals owned by Indian Tribes and individual Indians. The Branch is responsible for legal matters related to the acquisition and management of lands held in trust for the benefit of Indian Tribes and individual Indians; the management of the trust assets, including probate, and the use, leasing, sale, and conservation of trust assets such as forest and range lands; breach of trust and land claim litigation; environmental issues arising in connection with trust lands, and the protection and preservation of tribal cultural resources.

(3)   The Branch of Tribal Government and Alaska has responsibility for legal matters related to BIA tribal governmental programs and activities. In addition, the Branch is responsible for tribal status, treaty rights, reservation boundary, zoning, and taxation disputes; issues concerning Federal, State, and tribal jurisdiction; tribal courts and law enforcement and implementation of the Indian Civil Rights Act.

(4)   The Branch of General Indian Legal Activities has responsibility for legal matters related to BIA and BIE programs and activities other than those assigned to other branches. These matters include gaming, self-determination and self-governance, education, roads, social services, and economic development.

The **Division of Land and Water Resources** is responsible for legal matters related to the programs and activities of BOR and BLM, other than legal matters concerning BLM's mineral programs. The Division is also responsible for asserting, on behalf of all of Interior's bureaus, affirmative claims seeking reimbursement under the Comprehensive Environmental Response, Compensation and Liability Act (CERCLA) for costs incurred by those bureaus in remediating contamination on bureau lands. The Division also defends the bureaus in contribution actions asserted against them under CERCLA and other laws. In addition, the Division provides legal assistance and counsel to the Assistant Secretary - Water and Science; the Assistant Secretary - Land and Minerals Management; and, with respect to matters concerning operation of the Department's Central Hazardous Materials Fund, the Assistant Secretary - Policy, Management and Budget. The Division has an Associate Solicitor and three branches, each headed by an Assistant Solicitor.

(1)   The Branch of Public Lands has responsibility for legal matters related to BLM land management functions, including land acquisitions, disposals, surveys, boundaries, withdrawals, classification, rights-of-way, trespass, land titles, land use planning, grazing, forest management, wildland fire issues, law enforcement, and wilderness.

(2)   The Branch of Water and Power has responsibility for legal matters related to BOR programs and activities, including contracting for water delivery; repayment, and operation and maintenance; hydropower development; water research and technology; water policy; and water rights.

(3)   The Branch of Environmental Compliance Response has responsibility for legal matters related to cost-recovery and cost-avoidance involving cases funded from Interior's Central Hazardous Materials Fund. The Branch also has responsibility for legal assistance and counsel with respect to issues of environmental compliance that arise under numerous state and federal laws at Interior's facilities, as well as environmental liabilities that arise during real property transactions. The Branch also works closely with U.S. Environmental Protection Agency and other agencies in promoting the redevelopment of Brownfield sites; encouraging the cleanup of mixed ownership sites (private and public lands); and facilitating the remediation of formerly used defense sites. The Branch also coordinates its response activities with Interior's Natural Resources Damage Assessment and Restoration Program.

The **Division of Mineral Resources** is responsible for legal matters related to the programs and activities of BOEM; BSEE; OSM; USGS, other than those related to its Biological Research Division; and BLM's mineral programs. The Division is also responsible for legal services pertaining to programs and activities of the Department related to the Law of the Sea and international law affecting marine minerals, pollution, and related matters. The Division provides legal assistance and counsel to the Assistant Secretary - Water and Science and the Assistant Secretary - Land and Minerals Management.

(1)   The Branch of Petroleum and Offshore Resources provides legal services to BOEM and BSEE. It is responsible for legal matters related to Outer Continental Shelf mineral and energy leasing and the regulation of operations on such leases; establishing financial terms in leases and the grant of relief therefrom, and the

requirement of bonds for the performance of lease obligations; oil spill response planning and oil spill financial responsibility for offshore facilities; and international issues relating to OCS mineral extraction, including establishment of maritime boundaries. It also is responsible for legal advice related to the BLM fluid minerals program (with the exception of geothermal resources), and BLM matters associated with oil shale and tar sands. Attorneys in the Branch of Petroleum and Offshore Resources represent BLM, BSEE and BOEM in the adjudication of oil and gas litigation before the Interior Board of Land Appeals.

(2)   The Branch of Onshore Mining and Reclamation has responsibility for legal matters related to the minerals programs (including geothermal resources) of BLM and USGS, other programs of BLM and USGS, including development and extraction, environmental regulation and protection, reclamation, remediation, and issues arising from both active and abandoned mining activities, but excepting matters pertaining to oil, gas, helium, oil shale, and tar sands.

(3)   The Branch of Surface Mining has responsibility for legal matters related to OSM programs and activities, including regulatory programs, enforcement and collections, and abandoned mine land reclamation.

The **Division of Parks and Wildlife** is responsible for legal matters related to the programs and activities of NPS, FWS, and the Biological Research Division of the USGS. In addition, the Division provides legal assistance and counsel to the Assistant Secretary - Fish, Wildlife and Parks and the Assistant Secretary – Water and Science. The Division has an Associate Solicitor and three branches, each headed by an Assistant Solicitor.

(1)   The Branch of National Parks has responsibility for legal matters related to NPS's programs and activities and for legal matters related to the programs and activities of NPS's National Capital Region and the United States Park Police.

(2)   The Branch of Fish and Wildlife has responsibility for legal issues related to the programs, activities, and policies of Interior and FWS concerning conservation, the preservation of migratory birds, fish, other kinds of endangered species, game and marine mammals, and their habitats throughout the United States, its possessions and territorial waters; the protection, management, and use of natural and cultural resources within the National Wildlife Refuge System; and interaction and liaison between Interior and other Federal and state agencies, foreign countries and international organizations.

(3)   The Branch of Environmental Restoration has responsibility for the resolution of legal problems which involve the programs, activities, and policies of Interior and its various agencies, when related to natural resource restoration.

The **Indian Trust Litigation Office** (ITLO) within the Immediate Office of the Solicitor, Washington, DC, provides legal counsel and defends litigation filed in federal courts throughout the country against the Department by individual Indians and Indian tribes that implicates the Secretary's trust duties with respect to trust fund accounting, trust fund management, and management of non-monetary natural resource trust assets. ITLO has primary responsibility for matters filed in the United States Court of Federal Claims seeking money damages under 28 U.S.C. § 1505 for alleged breaches of fiduciary trust.

Regions and Field Offices. To the extent practicable, legal services are provided based on bureau regional boundaries, rather than SOL regional boundaries. Because regional boundaries vary from bureau to bureau, the actual areas served by the Solicitor's Regional and Field Offices overlap to a considerable extent, with the result that more than one Regional or Field Solicitor's Office may handle legal matters for different bureaus within a single state. In addition, Regional and Field offices are responsible for legal matters arising in Interior's offices within their jurisdiction, including all elements of the Office of the Secretary, the Assistant Secretary – Policy, Management, and Budget, and organizations affiliated with Interior.

     A. The **Alaska Region** is responsible for legal matters involving all bureaus except OSM and BOR in Alaska. The Regional Office is located in Anchorage, Alaska.

     B. The **Northeast Region** is responsible for legal matters involving all bureaus except BIA in Connecticut, Delaware, Maine, Maryland, Massachusetts, New Hampshire, New Jersey, New York, Pennsylvania, Rhode Island, Vermont, Virginia, and West Virginia; legal matters involving all bureaus except NPS in Illinois, Indiana, Michigan, Minnesota, Ohio, and Wisconsin; and legal matters involving specific bureaus in Iowa (BIA, FWS, and USGS), Kentucky (OSM), Missouri (FWS), Nebraska (BIA), North Dakota (BIA), South Dakota (BIA), and Tennessee (OSM). The Regional Office is located in Newton Corner, Massachusetts, and Field Offices are located in Fort Snelling, Minnesota, and Pittsburgh, Pennsylvania.

     C. The **Pacific Northwest Region** is responsible for legal matters involving all bureaus in Idaho, Oregon, and Washington; and legal matters involving the BIA in southern Alaska (Metlakatla) and northwestern Montana (Flathead Indian Reservation). The Region also handles legal matters for the Pacific Northwest Region of BOR extending into northwestern Montana, and for Region I of the FWS, it handles legal matters in Hawaii and the Pacific Islands. The Regional Office is located in Portland, Oregon, and a Field Office is located in Boise, Idaho.

     D. The **Pacific Southwest Region** is responsible for legal matters involving all bureaus in California and Nevada; and legal matters involving specific bureaus in Alaska (OSM and USGS), Hawaii (NPS and USGS), Idaho (OSM), Oregon-Klamath Basin (BOR), Pacific Islands (NPS and USGS), and Washington (OSM and USGS). The Regional Office is located in Sacramento, California, and a Field Office is located in San Francisco, California.

E. The **Intermountain Region** is responsible for legal matters involving all bureaus except FWS and OSM in Utah; legal matters involving all bureaus except FWS, NPS, and OSM in Arizona; legal matters for BOR in Nevada and California (BOR Lower Colorado Region) and Colorado, New Mexico, and Texas (BOR Upper Colorado Region); legal matters for BIA in Nevada (BIA Eastern Nevada Field Office and Western Nevada Agency) and New Mexico (BIA Navajo Regional Office shared with the Southwest Region); and legal matters for BLM in Nevada (shared with the Pacific Southwest Region). The Regional Office is located in Salt Lake City, Utah, and a Field Office is located in Phoenix, Arizona.

F. The **Rocky Mountain Region** is responsible for legal matters involving the BLM National Operations Center (NOC) nationwide and all legal matters involving the BLM in Colorado, Montana, Nebraska, North Dakota, South Dakota, and Wyoming; all legal matters involving the BOR Denver Office and the BOR Great Plains Region (located east of the Continental Divide in Colorado, Wyoming, and Montana, and in Kansas, Nebraska, North Dakota, Oklahoma, South Dakota, Texas); all legal matters involving FWS Region IX in Colorado and FWS Region VI (Colorado, Montana, North Dakota, South Dakota, Utah, and Wyoming); legal matters involving the Office of Natural Resources Revenue (ONRR) and legal matters involving BOEM and BSEE in Colorado; legal matters involving the Interior Business Center (IBC) in Colorado; legal matters involving the NPS Denver Service Center, NPS WASO in Colorado, the NPS Midwest Region in Arkansas, Iowa, Indiana, Illinois, Kansas, Michigan, Minnesota, Missouri, Nebraska, North Dakota, Ohio, South Dakota, and Wisconsin, NPS concessions contract matters for the Midwest and Intermountain Regions; and all other legal matters involving the NPS Intermountain Region in Colorado, Montana (with the exception of Big Hole Battlefield—Nez Perce), and Wyoming; all legal matters involving the BIA in Montana (with the exception of the Flathead Indian Reservation) and Wyoming; all legal matters involving the Central Region of the USGS; and all legal matters coordinated through OSM Western Region. The Regional Office is located in Lakewood, Colorado and a Field Office is located in Billings, Montana.

G. The **Southeast Region** is responsible for legal matters involving all bureaus in Alabama, Florida, Georgia, Kentucky, Mississippi, North Carolina, Puerto Rico, South Carolina, Tennessee, and the Virgin Islands; legal matters involving all bureaus except BOEM and BSEE in Louisiana; legal matters for specific bureaus in Arkansas (FWS and OSM), Connecticut (BIA), Illinois (OSM), Indiana (OSM), Iowa (OSM), Kansas (OSM), Maine (BIA), Massachusetts (BIA), Missouri (OSM), New York (BIA), Oklahoma (OSM), Rhode Island (BIA), Texas (OSM), and Virginia (BIA, BLM, and OSM); and legal matters for specific NPS programs in select states in the Region. The Regional Office is located in Atlanta, Georgia, and a Field Office is located in Knoxville, Tennessee.

H. The **Southwest Region** is responsible for legal matters involving all bureaus in New Mexico, Oklahoma, Texas, and on the Navajo Reservation; and legal matters involving specific bureaus in Arizona (FWS, and OSM), Colorado (BIA), Illinois (OSM), Kansas (BIA, BLM, BOEM, and BSEE), Louisiana (BOEM and BSEE), and Missouri (BIA). The Southwest Region also is responsible for legal matters involving the BIA's Office of Law Enforcement and the Office of Facilities Management and Construction, the BIE, and the Office of the Principal Deputy Special Trustee. The Regional Office is located in Albuquerque, New Mexico, with a unit in Santa Fe, New Mexico, and a Field Office located in Tulsa, Oklahoma.

ETHICS OFFICE ACTIVITY

Activity: Ethics Office
(Dollars in Thousands)

	2013 Actual	2014 Enacted	2015			Change from 2014 (+/-)
			Fixed Costs & Related Changes (+/-)	**Program Changes (+/-)**	**Budget Request**	
Ethics Office	1,495	1,495	+ 243	0	1,738	+ 243
FTE	*8*	*8*	*0*	*0*	*8*	*0*

The 2015 budget request for the Ethics Office is $1,738,000 and 8 FTE.

PROGRAM OVERVIEW

The Departmental Ethics Office (DEO) is responsible for overseeing Interior's statutorily mandated ethics program, and derives its authority directly from the Secretary, who by regulation, is the head of the agency's ethics program. The DEO is responsible for implementing the laws, executive orders, regulations and departmental policies concerning conflicts of interest and employee responsibilities and conduct (5 C.F.R. § 2638.201-202). The DEO is unique within the Office, as it has programmatic responsibilities, as well as the rendering of legal advice.

The DEO is headed by a Director, who is also the Designated Agency Ethics Official (DAEO). The DAEO is delegated the responsibility to manage and coordinate Interior's Ethics program (5 C.F.R. § 2638.202-203). The DEO also ensures the implementation of and compliance with the Ethics in Government Act of 1989, other statutes with ethics provisions, Executive Order 12674: *Principles of Ethical Conduct for Government Officers and Employees,* government-wide ethics regulations, and Interior's supplemental ethics regulations and policies governing employee conduct.

The DEO develops departmental ethics policy and strives to provide every Interior employee the proper counseling and technical assistance to help them with the ethics and conduct issues they may face as entrusted public servants. The Office seeks to integrate leadership and ethical concepts into everyday decision making in order to foster and maintain high ethical standards for Interior employees and to ensure that employees incorporate an awareness of the ethics rules and regulations into their day-to-day management practices.

The DEO provides direct services to all employees: within the Immediate Office of the Secretary, under the Assistant Secretary for Policy, Management and Budget, employees within the SOL as well as all political employees. Along with this program requirement, the DEO is responsible for providing oversight and technical assistance to Interior's eight bureaus to ensure that each of the bureaus' ethics programs are in compliance with all applicable ethics laws, executive orders, and regulations (5 C.F.R. § 2638.202).

The DEO performs a number of tasks required by law or regulation. Additionally, the DEO provides other, broader assistance in a variety of Interior initiatives to ensure that attention is paid to whether a particular course of action is prudent and in concert with ethics laws and regulations at large. Comprehensive attention to both types of responsibilities is critical to maintaining a robust ethics program throughout Interior.

At the request of the Secretary of the Interior and with the support and direction of the Solicitor, the Director of DEO reviewed the Office of Government Ethics (OGE) Ethics Program Model Practices to determine what practices Interior already utilized and to determine which additional model practices Interior could or should implement. Of the eighty Ethics Program Model Practices, Interior was already utilizing sixty, although some enhancements and improvements are needed.

Based on this review, the Director developed a strategic action plan on how to implement the remaining twenty Ethics Program Model Practices. While incorporating new Model Practices into Interior's ethics program and enhancing other practices it is essential to continue the technical competence of the ethics program. In addition to that initial action plan, and in implementing the Secretary's Secretarial Order directing the enhancement of the Department's Ethics Program, the Director has updated the action plan and continues to develop new initiatives to foster a stronger ethical climate with partners, industry and other non-federal entities. Some of the Model Practices that have been incorporated include:

> The DEO has increased its liaison efforts with the OGE and has served as a member of the OGE Leadership initiative focus group. Additionally, the DEO is a member of the Ethics Resource Center and the Ethics Compliance Officers Association.

> The DEO, as part of its efforts to increase training initiatives, is a member of the Interagency Ethics Council task force on training. The DAEO and Alternate Agency Ethics Official and other ethics officials from the DEO presented ethics sessions at the Solicitor's Management Conference, at politicals' meetings, and several other conferences. The DEO will focus on several training initiatives based on the Departmental Ethics Training Plan including:

- Personal appearances by Senior Leaders at training;
- Preparing effective decision making modules for training to enhance the ethics culture;
- Asking managers to discuss ethics related issues with their staff at staff meetings and other work settings;
- Identifying trends of ethics violations and publicizing consequences from ethical lapses;
- Use media accounts to showcase what happens to those who violate the laws;
- Focusing on training the 14 guiding principles of ethics;
- Soliciting feedback on training from employees; and

- Training ethics officials, branching out their training into effective decision making and an ethical culture.

The DEO was trained in program reviews and conducted an assessment of the BIA ethics program, similar to an OGE program review. The results of this assessment assisted in determining additional processes and systems to be implemented and incorporated into the BIA ethics program. There will continue to be assessments of the bureau ethics programs by the DEO. Bureaus Ethics Counselors will also receive program review training to properly execute their oversight role.

To improve the financial disclosure process, the DEO procured and is in the process of implementing an electronic system of employee filing and DEO review. The DEO is participating in multi-agency initiatives overseen by the Office of Government Ethics, such as the Ethics Counselor Certification Program and the Benchmarking Project to develop ethics program assessment tools. The DEO is reviewing DOI supplemental ethics regulations to determine appropriate revisions to further assure the highest level of ethical culture at DOI.

REQUIRED FUNCTIONS

➢ Oversight and Technical Assistance to Bureaus: Not only is the DEO responsible for performing ethics functions for a broad spectrum of employees, it is also responsible for ensuring that Interior's bureaus are properly administering their ethics programs. The regulations require that the DAEO administer a program for periodic evaluation of the ethics program and its components. Currently, the DEO meets this responsibility by convening monthly meetings with the bureaus' headquarters ethics contacts to ensure consistency in the management of the program. Additionally, the DEO has utilized contract services to perform program reviews of the bureaus. The DEO provides, live workshop training on topics important to the consistent management of the bureaus' ethics programs. The DEO will conduct a program review as part of the oversight responsibility of the office.

➢ Presidential Appointments: The DEO plays a critical role in the clearance process of nominees to Presidentially Appointed-Senate Confirmed (PAS) positions. The DEO reviews financial documents, consults with the nominees, and recommends and drafts appropriate recusals or authorizations to allow the nominees to perform their duties without actual or apparent conflicts of interest. Key in this process is the coordination with the White House Counsel's Office, and the OGE. Additionally, the DEO works with Interior's Office of Congressional and Legislative Affairs to prepare nominees for their committee hearings and assists in the drafting of responses to any questions committee members may have. In a Presidential transition year, additional time is spent coordinating and ensuring compliance with the financial disclosure requirements for all political appointees, training these employees, and providing individual counseling on a range of ethics topics essential to the appropriate performance of their official duties.

➤ Financial Disclosure: The DEO is responsible for ensuring that the public and confidential financial disclosure reporting requirements are met. Both levels of financial disclosure require the administration of tracking systems for the collection, review, and certification of the forms in accordance with the time frames set out by regulation (5 C.F.R.§ 2634.601-607; § 2634.901-909). Additionally, any remedial action required as a result of review and certification of these forms must be administered by the DEO or respective bureau ethics program. Such remedial actions include divestiture, recusals, or authorization, all of which require a determination in accordance with criminal statutes and administrative regulations. Department-wide, there are approximately 13,000 filers of financial disclosure forms. All forms require technical as well as more stringent financial conflict of interest review and certification. The DEO is responsible for certifying all financial disclosure forms of employees in the Immediate Office of the Secretary, under the Assistant Secretary for Policy, Management and Budget, employees in the Office of the Solicitor and all Interior political employees. PAS employees' financial disclosure forms are certified by the DAEO and forwarded to OGE for final certification.

➤ Training: The DEO is responsible for providing new employee ethics training as well as annual training for all filers of the confidential and public financial disclosures. All report filers are required to receive annual training. The administration of the ethics training program is in accordance with 5 C.F.R. § 2638.701-708. The DEO is responsible for providing guidance and training for all bureau ethics counselors to ensure consistency in the advice and counseling provided to employees.

➤ Counseling: As required by 5 C.F.R. § 2638.203, the DEO is responsible for maintaining a system for counseling employees on all ethics matters, including interpretations of the criminal financial conflict of interest statutes, the post-employment statute, as well as all standards of conduct regulations (both government-wide and agency-specific). Such systems must include adequate documentation of questions raised and advice rendered to provide employees with advice, but also for purposes of audit and evaluation by the OGE, or in support of an investigation of alleged violations by the Office of Inspector General. The DEO is responsible for providing guidance and counseling to ethics counselors and general employees on any changes to the ethics rules and regulations.

➤ Liaison Role: The DAEO is required to be Interior's liaison with the OGE for all matters relating to the management of the ethics program (5 C.F.R. § 2638.203(b)). The DAEO and ethics staff performs this role with the White House Counsel's Office, as well as with the Office of Special Counsel.

NECESSARY FUNCTIONS

There are a number of necessary functions performed by the DEO to meet its responsibilities and to ensure a robust and proactive ethics program, which includes prevention, education, identification of violations, and coordination of enforcement actions. Among these necessary functions are:

➤ Act as liaison and technical advisor to the Office of Inspector General (OIG).

➤ Compile Department-wide annual reports to be submitted to the OGE.

➤ Participate in the work of the Deputy Chief Human Capital Officer workgroup, to ensure that Interior's human resources responsibilities include attention to ethics, i.e., working to include ethics management performance standards in supervisors and ethics counselors' position descriptions.

➤ Serve on several Department-wide initiatives, such as donations of gifts policy; appropriate identification of ethics considerations for volunteers and special government employees; and the Agency Emergency Preparedness Team.

➤ Work with the Division of General Law on the Federal Advisory Committee Act issues that raise ethics questions, such as the proper designation of members as either representatives or special government employees, and ensuring the administration of financial disclosure requirements for those designated as special government employees.

➤ Ensure an adequate system for responding to FOIA requests as well as requests for documents or other technical assistance from Congressional Committees.

SECTION 404 COMPLIANCE

Public Law 113-76, the 2014 Consolidated Appropriations Act requires disclosure of program assessments used to support Government-wide, departmental, or agency initiatives or general operations.

> *SEC. 404. The amount and basis of estimated overhead charges, deductions, reserves or holdbacks, including working capital fund and cost pool charges, from programs, projects, activities, and subactivities to support government-wide, departmental, agency, or bureau administrative functions or headquarters, regional or central operations shall be presented in annual budget justifications and subject to approval by the Committees on Appropriations of the House of Representatives and the Senate. Changes to such estimates shall be presented to the Committee on Appropriations for approval.*

The administrative costs for this Office will be displayed in two components – **External Administrative Costs**, and **Bureau Billing for Client Support** for reimbursable attorney positions funded by clients.

External Administrative Costs – the following table illustrates external administrative costs paid to Interior and other agencies to support Department-wide activities such as IT security, architecture, and capital planning; training through DOI University; telecommunications; finance and accounting services; building security; mail room; and enterprise licenses.

External Administrative Costs (Dollars in Thousands)	FY 2013 Actual	FY 2014 Estimate	FY 2015 Estimate
Interior's Working Capital Fund			
Centralized Billings	3,654.5	3,890.0	3,501.4
Direct Billings	979.7	1,022.5	979.5
Total	4,634.2	4,912.5	4,480.9

> ➢ **Bureau Billing for Client Support** - A number of client bureaus and offices within Interior have requested assistance beyond the level of services this Office is generally able to provide. The client generally has identified a special project needing legal services of limited duration but some urgency. In these instances, the Office typically hires one or more attorneys on term appointments for the duration of the project, and the Office enters into a reimbursable support agreement with the client to cover the cost.

The table below illustrates the indirect overhead costs for reimbursable attorney positions funded by clients. The indirect overhead costs reflects a pro rata portion of operating costs which includes space, telecommunications, postage, courier services, supplies, printing, copying, computer equipment, law books, IT services, automated legal research services, and external administrative costs.

Bureau Billing for Client Support (Dollars in Thousands)			
	FY 2013 Actual	FY 2014 Estimate	FY 2015 Estimate
Attorney salaries and benefits	13,844.0	13,830.0	13,830.0
Reimbursable attorney overhead	2,858.0	2,838.0	2,838.0
Total	16,702.0	16,668.0	16,668.0

In addition to reimbursements for staff positions and some related expenses, client bureaus continue to fund a portion of the Office's travel. Consistent with the understanding developed with the Appropriations Committees, travel related to litigation and other core Office functions is paid out of the SOL appropriation, but clients fund some travel for our attorneys to provide client training, attend meetings, and for other matters not involving core Office functions.

Pursuant to CERCLA, as amended (42 U.S.C. 9601, et seq), the Federal Water Pollution Control Act (Clean Water Act), and the Oil Pollution Act (OPA) of 1990, (U.S.C. 101-380), the Office will receive funding, funding level yet to be determined, from the Natural Resource Damage Assessment and Restoration (NRDAR) Fund for NRDAR-related travel and work.

OFFICE OF THE SOLICITOR
EMPLOYEE COUNT BY GRADE

	FY 2013 Actual	FY 2014 Estimate	FY 2015 Estimate
Executive Level IV	1	1	1
SES	18	20	20
Subtotal	**19**	**21**	**21**
GS-15	96	98	97
GS-14	202	202	201
GS-13	25	28	27
GS-12	17	17	17
GS-11	18	22	22
GS-10	1	1	1
GS-9	9	12	11
GS-8	9	9	9
GS-7	16	16	15
GS-6	3	3	3
Subtotal	**396**	**408**	**403**
Total employment (actual & estimates)	**415**	**429**	**424**

OFFICE OF THE SOLICITOR
PROGRAM AND FINANCING
(Dollars in Millions)

Identification Code 14-0107-0	2013 Actual	2014 Estimate	2015 Estimate
Obligations by program activity:			
0001 Direct program	62	66	66
0801 Reimbursable program activity	13	19	19
0900 Total new obligations	75	85	85
Budgetary resources:			
Budget authority:			
Appropriations, discretionary:			
1100 Appropriation	66	66	66
1130 Appropriations permanently reduced	-3	....	....
1160 Appropriation, discretionary (total)	63	66	66
Spending authority from offsetting collections, discretionary:			
1700 Collected	10	19	19
1701 Change in uncollected payments, Federal Sources	2	....	....
1750 Spending auth from offsetting collections, disc (total)	12	19	19
1900 Budget Authority (total)	75	85	85
1930 Total budgetary resources available	75	85	85
Change in obligated balances:			
Obligated balance, start of year (net):			
3000 Unpaid obligations, brought forward, Oct 1 (gross)	6	5	5
3010 Obligations incurred, unexpired accounts	75	85	85
3011 Obligations incurred, expired accounts	1	....	....
3020 Outlays (gross)	-76	-85	-85
3041 Reoveries of prior year unpaid obligations, expired	-1	....	....
3050 Unpaid Obligations, end of year	5	5	5
3060 Uncollected pymts, Fed sources, brought forward, Oct 1	-2	-2	-2
3070 Change in uncollected pymts, Fed sources, unexpired	-2	....	....
3071 Change in uncollected pymts, Fed sources, expired	2	....	....
3090 Uncollected pymts, Fed sources, end of year	-2	-2	-2
Memorandum (non-add) entries:			
3100 Obligated balance, start of year	4	3	3
3200 Obligated balance, end of year	3	3	3
Budget authority and outlays, net:			
Discretionary:			
4000 Budget authority, gross	75	85	85
Outlays, gross:			
4010 Outlays from new discretionary authority	70	80	80
4011 Outlays from discretionary balances	6	5	5
4020 Outlays, gross (total)	76	85	85

OFFICE OF THE SOLICITOR
PROGRAM AND FINANCING
(Dollars in Millions)

Identification Code 14-0107-0	2013 Actual	2014 Estimate	2015 Estimate
Offsets against gross budget authority and outlays:			
Offsetting collections (collected) from:			
4030 Federal sources	-13	-19	-19
Additional offsets against gross budget authority only:			
4050 Change in uncollected pymts, Fed sources, unexpired	-2	. . . .	. . . .
4052 Offsetting collections credited to expired accounts	3	. . . .	. . . .
4060 Additional offsets against budget authority only (total)	1	. . . .	. . . .
4070 Budget authority, net (discretionary)	63	66	66
4080 Outlays, net (discretionary)	63	66	66
4180 Budget authority, net (total)	63	66	66
4190 Outlays net (total)	63	66	66

OFFICE OF THE SOLICITOR
OBJECT CLASSIFICATION
(Dollars in Millions)

Identification Code 14-0107-0	2013 Actual	2014 Estimate	2015 Estimate
Direct obligations			
1111 Personnel compensation: Full-time permanent	38	41	41
1121 Civilian personnel benefits	11	11	11
1231 Rental payments to GSA	3	3	3
1252 Other services from non-Federal sources	1	2	1
1253 Other goods and services from Federal sources	9	9	10
1990 Subtotal, obligations, Direct obligations	62	66	66
Reimbursable obligations			
2111 Personnel compensation: Full-time permanent	8	8	8
2121 Civilian personnel benefits	2	2	2
2210 Travel and transportation of persons	1	1	1
2253 Other goods and services from Federal sources	2	2	2
2990 Subtotal, obligations, Reimbursable obligations	13	13	13
Allocation Account - reimbursable:			
4111 Personnel compensation: Full-time permanent	....	3	3
4121 Civilian personnel benefits	....	1	1
4252 Other services from non-Federal sources	....	1	1
4253 Other goods and services from Federal sources	....	1	1
3990 Subtotal, obligations, Allocation Account - direct	0	6	6
9999 Total new obligations	75	85	85

OFFICE OF THE SOLICITOR
REIMBURSABLE POSITIONS
(Dollars in Thousands)

	FY 2012	FY 2013	FY 2014
Bureau of Indian Affairs			
Legal support, licensing of FERC projects	188	199	200
Legal support, probate and AIPRA issues	182	42	118
Legal support, BIE priority matters	22	207	238
Legal support, BIA ASIA matters	90	0	0
Legal support, BIA CADR issues	0	0	102
Legal support, BIA OJS matters	91	168	294
Legal support, BIA matters	99	123	194
Legal support, BIA Navajo Region	11	128	182
Subtotal	683	867	1,327
Bureau of Land Management			
Legal support, mining, rights-of-way, NEPA, CERCLA, FLPMA, NHPA, grazing, forest fire cost recovery, title issues, and recreational use of public lands	76	75	77
Legal support, SNPLMA, other special assignments on behalf of BLM	189	166	198
Legal support, public land, environmental oil & gas, and energy law	124	124	125
Legal support, NEPA relating to the EPAct of 2005	162	152	163
Legal support, land use planning; work related to FLPMA and BLM's regulations implementing FLPMA, NEPA, ESA, NHPA, and other statutes, regulations, and policies	316	181	184
Legal support, all issues related to land and mineral resources	473	445	508
Legal support, special assignments on behalf of BLM	187	211	196
Legal support, natural resources in Idaho	374	374	379
Legal support, including employment law, and other duties as assigned	293	0	0
Legal support, resources, personnel, and wildlife	39	70	73
Legal support, related to renewable energy	386	386	395
Legal support, renewable energy, other special assignments on behalf of BLM	530	261	178
Legal support, natural resources and minerals in New Mexico	75	75	75
Subtotal	3,224	2,520	2,552

OFFICE OF THE SOLICITOR
REIMBURSABLE POSITIONS
(Dollars in Thousands)

	FY 2012	FY 2013	FY 2014
Bureau of Ocean Energy Management			
Legal support, offshore minerals and renewable energy issues	311	344	202
Legal support, relating to offshore minerals	583	582	566
Legal support, relating to Alaska issues	50	133	192
Legal support, relating to offshore renewable energy issues	153	169	178
Subtotal	1,097	1,228	1,138
Bureau of Reclamation			
Legal support, stream adjudication and water rights issues	143	152	151
Legal support, water contracts, water rights issues, Klamath project issues, NEPA, and NHPA	159	151	158
Legal support, Lower Colorado Region to include Colorado River management and regulations, drafting and review of water contracts, water accounting issues, Indian water settlements	209	204	210
Legal support, Reclamation law, Indian water rights settlements, NEPA, CWA and ESA	109	0	0
Legal Support, Central Utah Project – Title II construction and Title III mitigation programs	183	178	184
Legal support, Boulder Canyon Project Act	152	167	185
Legal support, Bay Delta Conservation Plan (BDCP), Central Valley Project Improvement Act implementation, ESA, NEPA, CVP operations, San Joaquin River Restoration Program	206	196	203
Legal support, land management, contract reviews, water issues, ESA, NEPA, BBDCP, and San Joaquin River Settlement	203	47	214
Legal support, water rights, water quality, and contracts for the CVP, non-CVP projects in California and others in Nevada	208	216	217
Legal support, Great Plains Region water service contracts, land title, NEPA, Indian water rights settlements, and general water rights	159	155	171
Legal support, water rights	96	95	120
Legal support, general law, realty, and EEO/MSPB	0	79	163
Legal support, Yakima water projects	24	125	190
Legal support, realty, land management, cultural resources, NEPA, ESA, CWA, and Washington BOR projects	0	0	140
Legal support, BOR contract actions	20	0	0
Legal support, water and Klamath project issues	67	75	84
Legal support, including procurement, employment law, agreements, and any and all other legal support as necessary	70	537	100
Subtotal	2,008	2,377	2,490

OFFICE OF THE SOLICITOR
REIMBURSABLE POSITIONS
(Dollars in Thousands)

	FY 2012	FY 2013	FY 2014
Bureau of Safety and Environmental Enforcement			
Legal support, relating to the regulation of offshore mineral operations and enforcement of BSEE and DOI regulations	468	1,133	978
Legal support, project management relating to document discovery for Deepwater Horizon	187	32	0
Subtotal	655	1,165	978
Fish and Wildlife Service			
Legal support, civil service law, EEO, labor law, natural resource damage assessment, civil penalty, and environmental law issues	95	0	0
Legal support, FOIA, refuge management, and land acquisition matters	99	80	0
Legal support, Region 4 legal matters	43	43	47
Legal support, high priority refuge and ESA issues	187	184	192
Legal support, high priority realty issues	49	51	55
Subtotal	473	358	294
Interior Business Center			
Legal support, IBC contractual & acquisition services	1,036	792	509
Legal support, including procurement, employment law, agreements, and any and all other legal support as necessary	151	79	346
Subtotal	1,187	871	855
National Park Service			
Legal support, water rights issues	171	167	0
Legal support, civil service law, EEO, labor law, and tort law issues	95	188	197
Legal support, FOIA, partnership agreements, cultural and natural resources	99	98	0
Legal support, southeast region legal matters	119	141	141
Legal support, Elwha River Ecosystem and Fisheries Recreation Act	0	58	106
Legal support, NPS legal issues	58	176	192
Legal support, paralegal services	6	0	0
Legal support, concessions and leasing	192	216	222
Legal support, Everglades restoration	219	231	249
Legal support, including procurement, employment law, agreements, and any and all other legal support as necessary	251	373	519
Subtotal	1,210	1,648	1,626

OFFICE OF THE SOLICITOR
REIMBURSABLE POSITIONS
(Dollars in Thousands)

	FY 2012	FY 2013	FY 2014
Office of the Special Trustee for American Indians			
Legal support, Office of Special Trustee for American Indians	171	163	186
Legal support, trust policy and procedure projects	365	233	164
Legal support, Office of Special Trustee for American Indians	2,325	1,986	1,857
Subtotal	2,861	2,382	2,207
Office of Surface Mining Reclamation and Enforcement			
Legal support, OSM issues	214	202	217
Subtotal	214	202	217
Other Offices and Programs			
Legal support, NIGC legal issues	26	0	0
Legal support, ONRR royalty matters	433	191	195
Legal support, ONRR related matters	0	242	278
Legal support, ONRR ethics program administration	0	152	150
Legal support, ASIA CADR issues	9	102	0
Legal support, PMB budget issues	0	55	0
Legal support, FOIA Appeals	193	217	219
Legal support, WCF issues	9	182	184
Legal support, WCF issues reflecting cross-cutting matters arising from all DOI bureaus	0	176	178
Legal support, NRDAR	352	689	466
Legal support, HAZMAT compliance	1,043	941	1,174
Legal support, DOJ assignment	89	137	139
Subtotal	2,154	3,084	2,983
TOTAL REIMBURSEMENTS	**15,766**	**16,702**	**16,668**

FY 2013 Endangered Species Act (ESA) Payments - Department of the Interior

Case	Judicial District	Court #	Attorney Fees	Court costs	Payee	Payment date
Bonner County, et al. v. Ken Salazar, et al.	D. Idaho	12-567	$4,000.00	$0.00	Himebaugh, Daniel A.	7/11/13
Center for Biological Diversity, et al. v. Ken Salazar, et al.	N.D. Cal.	12-1767	$20,277.81	$722.19	Adkins-Giese, Collette	2/15/13
Center for Biological Diversity, et al. v. Ken Salazar, et al.	D. Ariz.	10-2130	$34,789.00	$0.00	San Carlos Apache Tribe	3/13/13
Center for Biological Diversity, et al. v. Ken Salazar, et al.	D.D.C.	12-1514	$8,420.00	$380.00	Atwood, Amy R.	5/30/13
Center for Biological Diversity, et al. v. Ken Salazar, et al.	D.D.C.	12-861	$55,397.00	$1,143.00	Atwood, Amy R.	9/5/13
Center for Environmental Science, Accuracy, and Reliability (Cesar) v. Ken Salazar, et al.	D.D.C.	12-1311	$6,750.00	$1,250.00	Smith, Ryan	8/29/13
Defenders of Wildlife, et al. v. Norton, et al.	D.D.C.	04-1230	$196,946.00	$3,054.00	Glitzenstein, Eric	1/4/13
Defenders of Wildlife, et al. v. Norton, et al.	D. Mont.	09-77	$380,000.00	$0.00	Harbine, Jenny	5/21/13
Margaret Copeland, et al. v. Ken Salazar, et al.	N.D. Miss.	12-5	$65,000.00	$0.00	Fink, Marc D.	3/21/13
Oregon Wild V. J. William McDonald	D. Or.	09-185	$10,443.00	$57.00	Carpenter Jr., William	12/13/12
Western Watersheds Project v. FWS	D. Idaho	10-229	$32,261.00	$739.00	Sudbury, Ryan	6/5/13
Western Watersheds Project v. FWS, et al.	D. Idaho	12-197	$97,000.00	$8,000.00	Rule, Lauren M.	6/3/13
Total ESA Payments			$911,283.81	$15,345.19		

FY 2013 Equal Access to Justice Act (EAJA) Payments - Department of the Interior

Case Name	Bur	Judge	Type	Amount	Hourly Rates	Venue	Citation	Appeal Status	Payment Date	Payee/Plaintiff's Attorney
Advocates for the West	BLM	Lynn Winmill	Court Decision	$79,214.00	$200-$300	D. Idaho	No. 4:09-CV-00507 BLW		9/12/13	Laurence J Lucas
American Wild Horse Preservation Campaign	BLM	Beryl A. Howell	Settlement	$55,000.00	$166-$187	D.D.C.	No. 1:11-CV-02222		12/18/12	Meyer Glitzenstein & Crystal
Drennon Construction & Consulting	BLM	Judge Sommers	Settlement	$80,000.00	$125-$400 Expert $125-$250	DOI Agency	CBCA 2391		5/7/13	OLES MORRISON RINKER & BAKER LLP
Wilderness Workshop, Natural Resources Defense Council, The Wilderness Society, Sierra Club	BLM	John L. Kane	Settlement	$98,000.00	$177-$180	D. Colo.	11-cv-1534		9/12/13	Earthjustice
William C. Carpenter for Oregon Wild	BOR	Ann Aiken	Settlement	$10,500.00	$125-$250	D. Or.	No. 6:09-cv-00185-AA		12/13/12	William C. Carpenter for Oregon Wild
Center for Food Safety & Public Employees for Environmental Responsibility v Salazar	FWS	James E. Boasberg	Settlement	$84,000.00	$185-$189	D.D.C.	1:11cv01457 (JEB)		5/13/13	Center for Food Safety
Conservation Force v. Salazar	FWS	John Bates	Court Decision	$39,740.40	$155-$181	D.D.C.	Civil No. 10-1057(JDB)	Decision at 615 F3d 508 (2010)	5/2/13	Conservation Force
Boardley v DOI	NPS	James S. Gwin	Court Decision	$74,554.74	$167-$175	D.D.C.	1:07-CV-01986		4/24/13	Michael Boardley
High Sierra Hikers Assn	NPS	Richard Seeborg	Settlement	$240,000.00	$172-$550	N.D. Cal.	Cv 09-4621 RS		4/17/13	Morrison & Foerster
Total				$761,009.14